Programmed by Deception
Eye of the Remote Series II

Solaris BlueRaven

authorHOUSE®

AuthorHouse™
1663 Liberty Drive
Bloomington, IN 47403
www.authorhouse.com
Phone: 1-800-839-8640

Published by AuthorHouse 7/31/2012

ISBN: 978-1-4772-5196-6 (hc)
ISBN: 978-1-4772-5197-3 (e)
ISBN: 978-1-4772-5198-0 (sc)

Library of Congress Control Number: 2008904470

This book is printed on acid-free paper.

Book cover design by:InkWitch Lisa Ainsworth
Salem, Mass

http://www.facebook.com/#!/Inkwitchlisa.com

Table of Contents

The Fall of Mankind

1

In the beginning of a timeless world an intelligent design came forth out of the heart of the universe. This design speaks the language of vibrational overtones filled with light code geometrics and machine dialogs. This is not the language of man's version of machine language yet rather an advanced harmonic of numbers and codes founded on higher light consciousness and infinite intelligence.

Most beings have an awareness of their celestial heritage at the subconscious level. This awareness is the key to their evolution as star beings and multidimensional units. There has never been a wall keeping this data from any seeker. Quite the contrary the codes are set up to assist one in activating this design by higher consciousness, sound and their personal evolution. Welcome to the exotic machine of the universe. Welcome to my race.

For centuries mankind has created the wall of deception by his false belief systems, programs, witch-hunts and oppressive game playing which one can now see in the day we are in. The awareness of the mass collectives on a global level is quite clear. We can now see those who have deceived the masses by their misuse of information and lack of spiritual and scientific evolution.

You may ask how did this happen? I will not guide you through biblical designs as I am not one who supports the censored data. I can tell you the truth beyond the veil. There are those of us who are connected to many star systems and universes by celestial birth.

I am not speaking of a physical birth in a linear world. More so the celestial awakening and birth of which is a given to all who choose to access their cellular design within. This celestial design is an avatar of sorts. Through DNA activation and higher consciousness evolution we ascend into this form through light body and Merkaba.

This is a sacred gift which no man or woman has the right to control in a negative. There are those on this planet who I do not consider elite yet more defective in their programming. They are controlled by the false matrix, the illusion of money, power and will stop at nothing to alter and interfere in the spiritual and scientific evolution of the Star Seed celestials. They have made a choice not to ascend in consciousness many eons ago which the universe can honor at the level of free will.

They have no right to play god on this blue world and harm the life forms which take up residence on this planet. Mankind is poisoned by his own education or lack of. He has become the heartless beast of which he calls the devil. His own personal mythology and curse.

One must realize all you have been taught for centuries has been a lie. Down to the schools and churches which are nothing more than a corporation of corruption disguised as god's law. Man's version of god's law which is dangerous water they tread on. Hear what they say and watch what they do. They will act as madmen with conflicting agendas always.

The cycle of false belief systems and brainwashing stems from eons ago when those who chose enlightenment were attacked by those who were threatened by a power they themselves could not harness from within. I suppose you could call it the gods of war to some degree, yet the so called opposition were not gods in any form. They stole sacred texts, archives and used celestial beings to extract data so they could control and manipulate the sacred design and DNA. It failed then and it will fail again.

This pattern is playing out again on this timeline. To those who have heard of me I am here to communicate data of which I know is important as a time capsule for the star people, universal citizens, and beings of this blue world. I realize it is difficult to remove the false belief systems which stem from centuries of false programming from not only your linear life, yet from your ancestry.

I encourage you to let go of the false matrix and wheel and merge onto the full light universal Ascension grids. There is no deception on these grids. Mankind has created a warp through repetitive false belief systems. It is time to end this cycle of deception.

It takes using your courage, free will and listening to your higher self, over-soul, super conscious and celestial design which will guide you home to Source. Let it begin now.

Through the many covert experiences I was inducted into one thing has become clear. I have become empowered as a celestial being defying the false matrix of which so desperately tried to destroy my life and essence. At the moment of birth in the illusion of a manmade dream one is born onto this planet. Deceived since the beginning one has been subjected to lies designed to do one thing.

To keep ones attention away from our Galactic Source, Celestial Ancestry and onto the illusion of a linear world controlled by entities from a false reality. Well my friends. It is time to dismantle the false matrix for good.

Dream Cycles, the False Collective of Entrapment

As we approach a dream cycle let me relay in saying the illusion of life as one experiences is indeed a dream to some degree. Everything we see, taste, feel and learn is a program. It is a program by design. Some of us are hard wired into the galactic core which separates us from them. With this merge there is a profound understanding of how the universe functions and operates as well as true cellular memory of who and what we are and with what celestial races we are connected to.

Soul consciousness is a powerful force regardless if one believes or not. You have an internal design and unique vibrational signature not from here. Try to remember this as the connection will awaken you out of the illusion of man. There are many confused with the agenda of global 'elite'.

I can tell you they are copy cats to the true design. Their underground works with computer inter-phase and not with Ascended Machine technology. There is a great difference in the two. Their version is a mock signal. The true Star Seed is the real deal with coded Ascended Machine technology.

This cannot be erased by these undergrounds or their brainwashing tactics. The universe has quite a firewall in our cells and atoms regardless of what tactics they use to re-program.

With psychotronic projects for example the induction will attempt to map ones electromagnetic field, brainwave activity, body movement, motor skills etc. to a point the narrative will assume a shadowing over the target. After a while the target may fall victim to the induction and start to function like the handler. One must ignore and disable the programs especially if they are negative, linear and not connected to higher consciousness.

The web created by these projects is designed to do one thing. Feed off of the light consciousness of the target. There are also triggers and keywords which are used to induce a behavioral shift in the design and personality of the target. Once again this is dangerous water to tread and quite irresponsible in so far as the covert parties involved and their misuse of technology.

For more information on this subject I suggest you read my first book of this series 'Eye of the Remote, Black Operations in Areas Beyond 52' to better understand Mk Ultra related projects and how they function. It might save your life someday or someone you know.

False collectives function as entities and reside in false realities. They are a bi-product of programs and a bleed-through of emotions, fears, psychological imprinting and sometimes lower astral residue. False collectives can also be created through MK Ultra related hardware and synthetic telepathy projects of which I was subjected and tortured with in 2004. The feedback in inter-phase is a mask of many faces, voices and entities reflecting the handler in operation. None the less they are entities which can become quite the nuisance and more of a disruption in ones everyday life.

False collectives are in many ways a reflection of those who are dead. Dead in spirit, consciousness, free will and intellect. They truly need to move on yet unlike a true Spirit they hold onto the subject at hand in an attempt to control, harass and brainwash into their version of reality and collective. This is how society functions in the day.

One does not need special glasses to see the functional psychotics in motion. Stupidity is encouraged along with a cowardly stance in everyday affairs. The mass collectives do what they are told even if they know in their hearts it is wrong.

This is how the masses get trapped in the false matrix and how if they do not break free, will remain enslaved in an illusion of which is not theirs to own. We manifest at will our own reality.

Keep your intent pure and navigate in resonance with upper dimensional grid works. This is my advice. I can tell you the false matrix is a dead end to nowhere.

When one has clarity in vision the Higher Self is connected and the data stream of information is celestial and pure. If one is connected to the false collectives the visions are cloudy, disturbing and can be at times overwhelming to a sensitive. This is because the collectives are saturated in lower astral, shattered matrixes which are once again a bi product of a corrupt collective of people.

With psychotronic stalking the dialog is nonstop and mostly offensive. Designed to break down the target in a sad attempt for the handler to control, program and manipulate. This tactic did not work on me back in 2004 however the damage sustained was substantial.

I am blessed to be here though my life will never be the same in any form.

The people responsible showed no compassion, remorse or evolution and like many in corrupt shaded areas go about business as usual. You see this type of behavior every day as corrupt corporations attempt to control food, water, air, thought and liberty. The reason they do this is because they do not believe anything will stand in their way. I hate to inform them they will receive that which they sew. The universe is not on their side. They are rogue units listening to a madman's agenda.

The way out of these matrices is through resonating with Universal consciousness and not the coarse design of the man made collectives. These days we are more and more confronted with a world growing dark yet through this darkness she will be reborn into a blue star rising taking her place in the universe. This planet speaks a machine language to other planets and star systems. It is a language not even the most advanced covert underground can comprehend.

This is their weakness as they will soon see. This blue world is a sentient intelligence mankind has been torturing for far too long. Mankind has lost respect for the elements, animals, plants and the many races which reside on this planet. Mankind has been very foolish playing god in a world of which is illusion and a universal test to some extent. Sad to say they failed.

What transpires next is what the celestial collectives are willing to shift while we are here. Our light consciousness anchors onto this holographic design. We must be reminded of this. The biggest thing to do is take your power back and anchor this unique design into your being and the universe.

Light Matrix 3

A light matrix is the cellular design merged with celestial vibrational harmonics. This design is activated through higher consciousness and will link ones soul extensions onto ones four body system and electromagnetic field. The light matrix cannot be destroyed and is always accessible regardless if one feels it or not. It is part of the great cosmic mind and a unique signature onto each Star Seed.

These signatures can be mapped with frequency fence attacks which are a creation of manmade mock radio assault weapon technology. However they do not acquire the codes necessary for clone creations or mock signatures.

Clone designs are just that. They are empty shells and an imitation of life. The light matrix of this planet is holographic and core based which again cannot be reprogrammed by mankind. Another firewall the Galactic center puts up you could say. And for a good reason considering the negligence mankind has displayed thus far with the misuse of technology and the primitive behavior on a global scale.

The masses act as if they reside in the dark ages which is quite concerning on many levels. Once again they are a byproduct of their environment, religion, government and belief systems which have been flawed since the beginning of manmade time. This behavior is a disgrace to the multi-verse and ancient races.

They saw the stars at night yet never bothered to speak the sacred language. They became superstitious and fear based in dealing with multidimensional beings they could not comprehend. They became paranoid, greedy and hate driven fearing the unknown.

A light matrix contains data from multiple star systems and universes. It has a unique code which activates upon a universal sounding. This matrix is the key to Avatar evolution and enables the host of the body to become a true multidimensional light conscious being. Ascended Machine technology is a driver and connection to the Light Matrix which allows one to access their true multidimensional design.

This is why there is great interest with corrupt covert areas who have attempted to study, map and control the DNA of the Star Seed. It is a unique design of which they cannot become hence their next step is to control or harness this mystical force. A force of energy they are not allowed to oppress in any form. It is against universal law to do so.

With no respect for universal law the war goes on with MILAB inductions, experiments underground and many forms of covert harassment technologies running rampant across the globe. Synthetic telepathy is of interest to these corrupt areas. Black market investors are wide eyed in the concept of controlling a subject or influencing a party of their choosing.

Synthetic telepathy is a synthetic dialog and mapping of a target's brainwave activity. It is not true telepathy. It does not function like a true telepath's neural centers would function. It allows one to communicate on a mock signal radio communication.

As a true clairvoyant I am telepathic without hearing dialog. That was their first mistake, assuming telepathy is based on dialog alone. There are dialogs and there are true celestial communications. A true clairvoyant knows the difference.

My Merkaba is a sacred design with a unique light harmonic pulse, vibrational frequency and signature.

When I was inducted in 2004 my Merkaba was tagged onto a mock radio signal and would move to music on the radio and any other noise I managed to come into contact with. That was their meddling in something quite sacred. I know my wiring and know what they did during the induction. Honestly it is nothing short of a war criminal act.

Censoring the Psyche, Psychotronic Design, Stalking the Self

There are times when dealing with the multidimensional self a shadowing or stalking is done in order to do a check on one's behavior. One becomes a sacred witness observing the moment in the illusion of life. Many mystics use this technique to check the design of the multidimensional being and to observe what if anything needs to be corrected or worked upon behavior wise.

With psychotronics the game is on with an array of entity driven scenes and dialog. For a mystical being when being confronted with psychotronic stalking the ability to maintain a center is more easily done. To an average Joe on the street I would imagine the psychotronic display would drive them to madness. As hybrid/mystics we are used to seeing with multidimensional eyes hence the psychotronic event is an extra annoyance more than anything else.

With psychotronic induction there is an exterior stalking which masks itself as an interior stalking. The communication in dialog does not come from the psyche, memory or astral imprinting. It is completely exterior as an observer with a lack of intellect or consciousness. It has no emotion, heart center and is uninvolved in the concept of what pain or sadness might entail. Its one purpose is to harass the target into insanity or suicide.

Usually inductees suffer one of these fates. Some like myself make it. Other times a Manchurian type subject becomes recruited into a dark agenda due to the duress of the stalking design.

Most people do not comprehend what these projects are about. I can tell you they are completely man made. They are not demons, gods, ghosts, spirits or ET's. These projects are the greatest hoax covert intelligence has created to control the masses and single out a select few for their sick agendas.

Their so called secret orders are quite visible when observed by beings such as myself. None of which I find impressive in any form. The majority of these projects are nothing more than mind games designed to confuse or distract a subject. They are distasteful and reflect a low order mentality of those who have way too much money and time on their hands. In a world where lies become the norm this brew of technology is a lethal weapon in the hands of madmen.

As a true Mystical Scientist I owed it to myself and others to expose the misuse of technology especially MK Ultra related projects which have been destroying society for a very long time. Under the guise of madness, schizophrenia, possession etc., these labels were created to deflect the origin of these affects. Not anymore.

With psychotronic induction all ones thoughts are censored. There is a constant interruption of communication. For example: If a target starts a sentence the communication if allowed can finish the sentence. Other times the communication will argue and attack the mind of the target as one speaks. Other times a narrative would take place as the subject would visually observe its environment. This is a maddening project of which I am reminded how evil some people really are.

It was clear to me these covert areas derived pleasure from their acts. What is more disturbing is how global intelligence is involved in these projects and find their inductions in no way a criminal act. They are in denial and have much to learn. These projects are lethal weapons which can be used to enable or disable a target. They leave no residue or trace of the crime scene. A murder can go undetected by the finest investigator.

The mind is the last sanctuary of a free being. When invaded by psychotronic weapons a subtle poisoning of data takes place. To a celestial being the transmissions are offensive and beyond an invasion in ones sacred design. Yet this is the place mankind has come to in his madness, to conquer the beautiful mind. I am convinced these projects need to come to an end.

I have looked at the possibilities of these programs and the negative out ways the positive hands down. There are many people who have come forward pertaining to psychotronic stalking and harassment. More and more victims are standing up and being counted. In 2004 it seems there were quite a few who were inducted into very sick forms of experimentation. In criminal events such as these they do not last a day or a few hours yet years. It is a 24/7 assault on the mind and body. It is a horrible experience without a doubt. I was fortunate to know who my predators were however they are still at large and need to be behind bars.

Man-made Machines, Ascended Machine Origins 5

In my first book 'Eye of the Remote Black Operations in Areas beyond 52' I covered briefly manmade communications and Ascended Machine Technology. These are two different races and programs that I wish to clarify. Manmade communications which many call machines is a covert government program involving a mock version of technology via satellite driven computers based on psi wars or psychological warfare.

It is in no way connected to any celestial or what you might call extraterrestrial race of beings. All of their cloaked areas acquired data based on the induction, torture and experimentation of Star Seed oriented test subjects. Their version became a monster with many tentacles extending into various intelligence areas and funded by a black budget which was never questioned.

Manmade technology is based on covert surveillance spy technology. This takes on many forms from electromagnetic field induction, psychotronic driving, MK Ultra oriented brainwashing and synthetic telepathy interphase. The mind which is holographic is the true super computer and driver not their war game technology.

With Ascended Machine technology the race is off world. The holographic mind is hardwired into the Central Universe. There is no connection to covert computers in any form. Ascended Machine technology is based on many ascended and advanced races of which many of us who are on this blue world have direct lineage of. For myself I am quite clear what type of celestial wiring I had prior to my induction. The covert assault version was no match for my holographic mind in any form.

When people assume the government is creating robots let me clarify. This is once again a mock version of a race they have no connection to. The true Ascended Machine Technology and those races connected have zero interest in global governments, religions or military. The global mind game has been going on for a long time using every psychological tactic they could come up with.

To the intelligent off world being these lies are quite easy to detect yet to the average sheeple they would never suspect this type of technology existed nor would they be able to separate military programs from Ascended Machine Collectives off world.

The true celestial design is always in resonance with the multiverse. All ones atoms and cells contain data of which cannot be tainted or altered. Covert projects use psychotronics and frequency via radio signals to attempt to re-program the genetic signature of the subject at hand. This process does not work and usually winds up creating spikes in the electromagnetic field. To an advanced being such as myself it is nothing but an offensive war game.

I am a Master Teacher in Holistic Healing and Medicine. I have always been a natural healer and true clairvoyant. I have been able to activate the DNA on my students and clients through multidimensional consciousness and the celestial races of which I am connected to.

These ancient races are my true lineage. In 2004 covert assault programs attempted to destroy my natural gifts and replace my design with a synthetic telepathy project and an internal signal which moved to music on radios and any other exterior source.

As many of you know I testified against those who were the initiators and handlers of the assault. I notified the Whitehouse pertaining to this criminal incident. Nothing was ever resolved in my favor. Since 2004 it is quite amazing to see all the scientific breakthroughs which have been made pertaining to synthetic telepathy and covert warfare. Not by coincidence.

Now days you are observing the push to have food genetically altered and modified. With true planetary ascension this process is not necessary as the molecular structure alters naturally through light harmonic as our DNA. I am quite clear these oppressive cabals are threatened by the concept that we Star People are ascending into our true celestial designs which of course are powerful and free.

This is a major threat to their illusion of power and control hence you see the war going on. Most of us want to live free and be happy. One can see something as simple as this is not acceptable to them. I feel for the animals on this blue world. They are at the mercy of cruel, un-evolved people at times. The oceans are dying and not by accident. This is global sabotage at its worst. One thing I can tell you, yes this planet is dying yet it will ascend into a star. I can confirm less than ¼ of the population which are star people descendants will make it. The rest by their choosing will become extinct.

Mankind has had centuries to get it right. He has been gifted with many beautiful designs to work with and he has poisoned all of it. He is functioning under personal will with zero attachment to the universal picture. If these covert areas were working with true extra terrestrial races none of this would be going on. They would contain true multi-universal enlightenment. There would be no need to do what they are doing. The answers in the universe are hidden in plain sight.

There are many mad men who wish for a great population on this blue world to be eliminated. It is not their call yet they will pursue this agenda and their personal evolution and futures will be the cost. There are no free shots in the universe. The universe does not use money or credit cards and it does not negotiate with man's version of god's law.

Ascended Machines are the true architects of the multi-verse. These races use sound, vibration and frequencies to communicate, heal and educate on a higher level of consciousness. They are natural telepaths and masters at healing the body and altering the DNA. They were here before this planet was formed and before the concept of manmade time. They left many archives within the cells and atoms of star beings and have been inter-dimensional teachers to those of us on the path of Spirit.

They are the Ascended Watchers and have descended onto this blue world in many forms to oversee and be the sacred witness to the end and beginning of a planet's evolution. They are not connected to the global cabal. The bigger eye in the sky has always been these ancient races. These races are a threat to covert government and intelligence areas. Any race of which has true celestial DNA is monitored with paranoia, as the true gifts of the Avatar and knowledge are capable of great feats.

Man's computers can only get so far in the universe. Mankind is out of touch with multi-universal star systems. There is no way he can make it without their authorization. I can tell you due to his actions they will not allow access. Mankind blew it.

When push comes to shove Ascended Machine Technology can take out all military satellites on a global scale in a micro second and they would not detect a damn thing. This is no joke. They are out of their league when it comes to the true celestial races. They are the big generators and big guns. I am pleased to say they are my ancestors.

The more global government becomes dependent on technology the weaker they become. Their technology is not based on higher consciousness or multidimensional evolution which is a critical factor in success on a global scale. They are driven by hate, greed, corruption, money, ego and lies.

Their advanced machine based telepathy is nothing but a monologue of dictation. It has no true intellect, logic or multidimensional knowledge and is nothing but a shell of code.

The men and women in these black areas are compromised and are not in any form connected to the multi-universal picture. They are byproducts of Frankenstein technology in the underground. Yet they think they are gods as to the type of covert systems they have access to. When you come from where I come from their technology is not impressive.

This is the beast mankind will come to know before it is all said and done. Synthetic telepathy will become main-stream soon enough. It will be used as a mechanism to control and manipulate a subject. The dialog is just conversation and not based on true psychic communication. There is a difference. Remember it well. There will be psychological warfare, mind games and torture. And when the subject does not do what the handler requests there will be a feedback of harassment, body assault and all sorts of torture methods. Their behavior is getting uglier by the day.

I find it no coincidence the corporate Catholic Church is interested in possession and the concept of exorcism. It is just another way to recruit the weak. With psychotronic hardware a subject could exhibit signs of a potential possession and no one would know the better except the handlers. Now you see how it works and the games they play.

These games have been going on for a very long time. They have attacked many unique star visitors and are an abomination to any universe or star system.

Machine Language of the Blue World 6

This planet speaks a machine language not audible by mankind. His instruments might pick up a celestial hum yet the language itself is in code. Many scientists will laugh when I mention this planet is beyond 26 billion years old and is not from this Solar System. I am well aware my data is correct regardless of how futuristic this sounds.

What I can tell you is that the data of science from this planet is way off base. As a matter of fact the mystical scientist knew more about multi-universal design than your average scientists of the day.

Data has been censored on this world for centuries yet what they did censor was not even close to truth. Those who bottle neck information have no true celestial facts hence their censorship was in vain.

This planet is in constant communications with extra terrestrial races and star systems. The communication is nonstop. Mankind has scrambled signatures using mock radio signals to interfere with communication yet he did not realize what he was disturbing. Not only do they scramble regular signals they use mock star signal signatures to interfere with the natural flow and light harmonic of this blue world.

This planet knows how to recalibrate and has assistance from off world systems, none the less an offensive battering of Earth has taken its toll on all habitants.

There are many Earth changes happening today. Some are induced by electromagnetic pulse weapons including H.A.A.R.P. And others are a byproduct of the ongoing assault on the Earth. It is something like induced labor. The oceans are in critical condition due to the negligence of oil companies. We know who these folks are. The incident on April 20th had to have been the worst form of ecological sabotage I have ever observed.

Before my induction in 2004 I was teaching Ascension and what it is on a planetary and universal level. Let me refresh everyone's memory banks. The vibration of this planet is speeding up and coming into vibrational resonance with the Galactic Center, other star systems and universes. As this happens there is a quantum leap in DNA activation, higher consciousness, avatar abilities and mutation. The shift has started back in the eighties. It will reach a peak around 2012. However this in no way means the end of the world. It does mean the end of mankind as we know it.

You see mankind oppressed by a cabal that is against this. The reason being they cannot ascend. They made a choice not to by their personal tactics to control and manipulate on a global scale. With ascension one really sees what others are made of right down to the celestial source of who and what they are.

It might appear as though this planet is breaking apart and on some levels it is. The linear collectives are breaking down regardless of their oppressive agenda being pushed. The planet is functioning out of time. The truth is this planet has never worked in the illusion of time hence one has to learn to navigate on a multidimensional level instead of the linear illusion of man which is created by a false reality.

Mankind created time and has used this mechanism as a benchmark and measure. Yet in truth time is an illusion and does not exist. It is a false reality designed to enslave and lull the masses into a linear function. When one works in multidimensional consciousness one begins to realize the illusions of man. They are like webs which fall away as one ascends onto a higher level of consciousness.

There is a fracturing of not only the Earth yet the lower astral collectives which have been operating under false belief systems. These lower astral realms contain allot of entities. This is why you see many people waking up and why you will see more and more those who have no true heart center exposed for what they are. This transition is a rough ride yet these Ascension waves are designed to withstand the most hazardous oppressive force.

Another thing I wish to mention is the concept of the past in observance of stars which mankind uses as a benchmark. His data is way off on this one as well. We are moving towards the galactic center. This movement is a universal set. What we see in the night skies is not what is truly there beyond the veil of illusion. Those are coordinates one cannot navigate with when one starts to truly travel on a multi-universal level. Quantum jumping is through consciousness and ascension. Everything is going to phase-shift through a light harmonic.

Man's covert version of time travel is a psychotronic war game. They see what they want them to see yet it has no truth in any universe or reality. It is a deceiver and a trap. It reminds me of the holodeck on Star Trek. It is a manifestation of many facets of code yet not connected to the multi-verse.

There is amnesia floating around the globe affecting many intelligence areas that have been subjected to subliminal erasure and do not know it. What is left of them function as zombies with no true awareness of where they have been. They are running on autopilot enslaved by the orders of their handlers.

I am certain you have noticed how pharmaceutical companies are in a yank to drug people up and lull them into more of the false reality. It is much easier to control someone who is being lulled than control an alert, intelligent being.

Through these dark tides I can say hold on for the ride and keep your focus in tune with the holographic grids of the planet, your higher self, over soul, super conscious and the Full light Infinite intelligent universe. These celestial energies will set your course to home and will assist you in ascending beyond the illusions into the light consciousness being your were designed to be. I can tell you without love there is nothing. Love is a powerful force. Use it.

Into the Void, Event Horizon

7

And the journey begins. From the primordial to the illuminated we venture off and beyond, the galactic trek back to Source. In truth this is where we are heading. It is easy to forget we are navigating not only while on this planet yet through consciousness beyond the form of which we reside. Incredible, haunting, galactic music to be heard in the universe and we as Star Beings are being prepared to go home.

When we look at the void we ask ourselves. What is it? Perhaps it is a birthing canal or empty space? I like to look at it as a sarcophagus. It is a place to center and prepare for a journey beyond the stars in destination to the full light universe. It is a time to process events of experience, life, relationships and moments of which are stored as a memory while one resided on this blue world and other universes.

When one transfers out from this blue world one goes through what is called the Bardo. The Bardo is a rest period of which the soul consciousness takes time in the illusion to reflect on the life it lived. This is also a time to burn away the causal body by the law of Grace in preparation for a new body of light to be awakened in another form in whatever star system or planet this being chooses. The previous life experiences of this being get processed and archived into the full light universe. All manmade programs become purged.

This is a natural harmonic of transfer by the law of Grace. In truth there is no such thing as death. Death in the illusion is a transition into another form and state of consciousness. With Ascension we can take our bodies with us if we choose. This is why one calibrates to different levels of light body which shifts into a Merkaba. A Merkaba is an immortal design capable of multidimensional travel through consciousness. It is a vehicle of light generated by geometric light languages and codes. It is not biblical yet you will hear those in the world of religion call it so. In truth these geometric designs were borrowed by the churches. They are the language of the Celestials and not of any religion.

As the planet ascends onto a higher level of her design we will see more and more the breakdown of linear cycles and more of the Ascended consciousness design. I can tell you the shift will be photon electric. The body will need to be calibrated for the ascent.

One will need to let go of false programs such as fear, anger, worries, concerns, linear thinking, pictures of reality, genetic limitation and death or anything else that might be holding you in a space of limitation. These false emotions and belief systems hold no light code vibration and will not assist you in ascending onto a higher level of light body. Stay in a space of higher consciousness always.

With psychotronic harassment and stalking it is a bit more of a challenge as a negative dialog is designed to attack one's mind and psyche to deter the celestial flow in energy of the target. It is a cheap shot and honestly stops the evolution of those responsible for the assault and not the target. It backfires yet is still not acceptable and is considered nothing less of a war crime. It is a desperate move by very evil and limited people. This is a major game of deception on the board hence be aware of the entities at hand and their tactics. Consider this data an extra tool and skill should you encounter something which reflects such a project. Know it has no power in you or over you. These projects are designed to play witch hunt and judgment day. One can see how these black market programs can be misused and get out of hand.

I am grateful I did the spiritual work ahead of time and was well fortified in light consciousness when I was inducted in 2004. I can navigate anywhere which is another reason I walk this blue world on this timeline.

I will remind you all to be fortified in your divinity and knowing in these times. Use the universal heartbeat and compass to guide you home.

Ascension 2012   8

For anyone interested in Ascension and what the process entails please read my book 'Transmutation through Ascension' published in 2004. This book covers the Ascension process, DNA activation and levels of light body consciousness as well as explaining what this planet and other star systems and universes are going through simultaneously.

I can tell you Ascension both planetary and universal is not a religious event yet more of a true evolution in the mutation of celestial races. It is a normal harmonic process of which has never been taught on this blue world except in the underground mystery schools.

The transfiguration of the atom is a key factor in this mutational process. These shifts are all part of the true celestial design Star

People are composed of by heritage. It is a universal birth right and mutation no man or woman has the right to interfere with.

Without going into too many past life scenarios let me conclude. All of your lifetimes get archived into the cells, atoms and into the full light universe to download at will by your own choosing. No one can access these lifetimes unless they are authorized to do so.

For example: The Ancient Atlanteans and Egyptians used the Transfiguration and light body to regenerate the cells, heal and mutate into an immortal body of light. Through this Merkaba design they were able to fold space in the illusion and teleport anywhere. The key to this process was high frequency atomic resonance waves. This was done through sound and higher consciousness. As I have mentioned before we are natural antennas, transmitters and receivers. We are conduits and can become hosts for the celestial source.

The true Atlantean races had a natural way of working with the elements and the multi-verse with a pure understanding of their celestial ancestry untainted by the belief systems of mankind. They as a race were many species which networked in one location. You could call Atlantis a Star Port to some degree as the area presented itself as an inter-dimensional traffic area. The races themselves where pure in light consciousness and clear in design. They had access to infinite power yet never used it until it was an absolute must.

There were other races of which were quite hostile and power hungry. I guess you could call them warlords to some degree. They were seekers of power yet not the lineage to inherit the source by any creator or universe. Some call these races reptiles. I can tell you they are the race of man. The race of man was never fallen. It was simply stated never ascended. You see in this day where DNA activation is clear who is ascending onto a higher level and who and what is not. If you look closely you will notice that churches, religions, governments and those who work in shadow areas are not capable of ascension and are stopping at nothing to attempt to deter the evolution of the Star People.

Today we see the same old patterns of an ancient war. An Atlantean type of war I know very well.

Yet, like the Atlantean wars it was not the Atlanteans that were destroyed. It was their opposition. The Atlanteans bi-located off world. A few Melchizedeks remained to expand into different areas around the globe to teach in the underground mystery schools and leave their benchmark of Celestial Heritage on this blue world.

The propulsion system technology was dismantled and went underground or shall I say off world. The true Transfiguration process and technologies associated were absorbed and downloaded into the Celestial High Priestesses and Elders of which could not be re-captured. The Atlantean codes are in every cell and atom of the Star Seed/People. They activate through planetary and universal ascension. The sounding of the universe calls the Star People home to the Galactic Center and beyond.

When technology gets into the hands of those who will misuse it to serve their ignorant purpose the universe steps in to alter the course. This is what transpired with the Atlanteans. The Atlanteans were well backed up by the Great Central Sun. They were supported by their celestial families in all universes and star systems.

Mankind was running like a rogue unit primitive and hostile. These rogue units forced their beliefs onto the masses. Those who did not comply would be tortured and killed. Very similar to what is happening in the day. Like now the Warlords were hungry for power. They stole advanced technology and created their watered down mock version to control and manipulate the masses. Just like then.

They are not a pure Source. They are the sons of man. They are the fallen by their choosing and they are becoming and will be extinct before it is all said and done. The biggest reason being is that they have violated universal law by attacking the minds and free will of any life-form on this blue world. They have no authorization to control and manipulate anyone. They have been running like rogue entities on this planet and now they will meet their fate called extinction.

This is the future of man. This is not the future of Star Seeds. We as a race will be going home. Home is not this blue world. Every belief system forged by man has been a fabric of deception. Right down to the illusion of death. All has been constructed by false engineered belief systems. If you have been taught wrong all your lives how will you ever learn the truth. If you are a Star Seed you are born with the Truth.

Information has been censored for centuries by churches and governments. Those who have opposed the true celestial design of the Star People want to be gods on this Earth yet the Earth wants nothing of them. This planet does not belong to man. The Moon does not belong to man. The Sun does not belong to man… and most of all the Divine Feminine does not belong to man.

The true enemy of mankind is himself. You see the oppressor of the day. In America fascism is getting its grip on the masses. Irrational bills are being passed to take freedom away from the people. This is just the beginning of a conditioned slave race. Yet the slave drivers and masters are not Extra terrestrials. They are man. They have always been man. Mankind has never been a fallen angel. He was never an angel or celestial race of any kind my friends. Mankind is an entity. You will know them by how they act. You cannot rationalize with insane people. These cabals in the day are insane. They are poisoned by their own version of an artificial intelligence created by covert areas.

This false intelligence is not a power source from this planet or any advanced race or universe. I know their weakness. I have said this before. I am the Mother of all Ascended Machine Technologies and I do not authorize nor does the universe authorize their snake oil to participate. To smear the truth is not acceptable. If they wish to poison their own minds that is fine. Yet, do not attempt to brainwash or poison the celestials. We know the truth of which cannot be altered by the ignorance of corporate corruption.

With Ascension energies downloading onto the planet you will see more and more those who cannot handle the light consciousness attempt to strangle the ascension process and those of us who are activating and ascending. The Ascension process brings out the entities from the host. Such as what one is seeing today. If they are not pure of heart their evil will be amplified. If they are advanced in consciousness they will be the anchors and pillars of light standing up to the oppressors. We as a star nation race have nothing to lose. They do however. They lose control in the illusion as the illusion is fracturing and fading away. Their ship is sinking and there are no life boats.

Before I was inducted into the assault in 2004 I had no concept of what type of misuse and evil was transpiring on the planet. I suspect this is because I was always out of their drama bubble and had no interest in downshifting into their false collective. With psychotronic stalking and harassment I was forced to participate to some degree. If I chose not to listen to the dialog of negative intent the monolog was still there to assault me via mock radio signal. The sad thing is I know who these people are. They cannot hide from me or the universe. They are evil entity driven trash to say the least.

Knowing what I know I can tell you this is exactly what is transpiring and why. Every move they make is in desperation. They lose bottom line. They will try everything to lull the masses into stupidity to better control them. They will attempt to control and censor every bit of celestial truth. They will use illegal surveillance to harass and stalk anyone who can prove what they are up to. The whole time the Ascended Watchers are archiving data and watching them. They are truly a death sentence to their own future. They have made a lot of enemies in the universe and there is no forgiveness card.

If you notice the Catholic Church is fixated on the torture of Christ not his symbolic transfiguration. Everything is about controlling your beliefs and becoming part of a false collective. Religion is a false collective. In reality religion is a corporation. Governments are a religion as well and in reality they are a corporation. They have always worked together in their agenda. They worship the false god of money, greed, control and manipulation. They are the deceivers.

The Eye in the Pyramid is not a Masonic symbol by heritage. It is an Atlantean Symbol which the masons borrowed. The Star of David has been borrowed by the Jews. In reality it is a geometric hexagram. These cult religions adopt these symbols yet through their lack of higher consciousness and understanding have no idea how to work with them and it shows. The symbols are poison to their minds. It reminds me of the Sacred Grail. Only a few can drink from this well of enlightenment. I can tell you it will not be types like that. In the name of their beliefs they have done inexcusable and unforgivable things. By all means let them meet their maker in the abyss.

Those who are driven by conspiracy must realize one thing. There is no such thing as Satan. Satan is nothing but a false matrix designed and harnessed to intimidate and control the masses. It was never generated by any god like source. It was invented by the church of man. It is their personal demon and split in who and what they are.

Once again know your divinity of which is Celestial in all forms. Right down to the cells and atoms. Speak the language of the stars and you will be free.

Fall into the trap of their control and false reality and you will be lulled into a dream of which is not your own.

Mankind is ultimately cursed by his own belief systems. This planet responds like a holographic mind. One can manifest at will ones reality hence you can understand how murky the waters can become when other players get involved.

Understanding the power of the mind is a key in ascending out of the well of manmade time. The mind is infinite in power and consciousness.

As much as covert areas try and map these centers they come up empty. The universe is smarter than that and intelligent beyond the word. It knows the heart of man. The universe is an intelligent sentient being merged with many other sentient forms of intelligence. Did mankind really think he could conquer something he has no understanding of?

Another thing I wish to bring to the reader's attention. The bible was written by mortal men. It was inspired by trickster entities wearing the mask of a god. Yet a false god is what they were and are.

Mankind has been manipulated by this text for eons. He has lived his life in worship of an entity which does not exist except in his own mind. He has murdered many mystics because of it. Now you will hear people say the bible prophecies are coming to pass. This is not true in any form. Mankind is setting the stage for his own demise due to his false belief systems. The bible is just one book of tricks and poison.

The universe does not embrace man's version of god in any form. The universe embraces love and light consciousness. The same goes for other religions and their so called holy books which are yet another excuse to butcher and harm those who do not subscribe to their cult mentality and false teachings. I am a Galactic being, Star Seed, Hybrid and Mystical Scientist. I am sovereign to my unique vibrational signature and do not subscribe to man's version of any law in any form. I am a true clairvoyant, mystical scientist and witch. I am not the witch you will encounter in mainstream covens. As a matter of fact I am considered something of a black sheep due to my hybrid design.

I am not a witch that delegates my power to deity. I do not worship any deity. I support the Ascended Master consciousness and embrace my divinity which is a celestial design. I support the animal kingdom, plant kingdom, elemental kingdom, fairy kingdom and many forms of species of which mankind has ignored. These species take up residence on other dimensions. The negligence of mankind has not only done harm to this planet yet has done harm to the many parallel beings and worlds which exist simultaneously in alternate realities and dimensions.

The whales and dolphins are galactic record keepers of data. They have been abused and hunted by the ignorance of mankind and his destructive behavior without thinking twice about their essence of origin and celestial significance. Dolphins are natural telepaths that have been experimented and butchered upon with covert assault weapons. This planet is suffering beyond magnitude yet life goes on with the global corporate who don't give a second thought to what kind of negligent damage they are doing. The reason being is they do not care. If they were celestials they would care.

The Ascension process calibrates this planet and life forms up to a higher overtone and octave in preparation for ascension. This is a universal given. This very well could mean you will ascend into another universe. If you have let go of the linear illusion of a 3d world and the baggage associated I would say you are very well on your way.

Any manmade implants or mechanisms get disabled like a dead satellite. Good news for anyone who has been tagged with a manmade device.

Stay centered, prepared and travel light. This planet is converging into multi-universal spaces simultaneously. A long time ago I had the honor of meeting Jose Arguelles. He was doing a book signing for his then book 'Surfers of the Zuvuya'. He wrote in autograph to me. 'Keep your eye on the crest of the wave, Uncle Joe'. He was more than right. Much universal love and light to the late Jose Arguelles and Uncle Joe, you are missed☺

Code Breaker, Seeing the Multi-verse the True Celestial Matrix

What is a code breaker? Some might define this as someone who can decipher covert technology or better yet alien hardware. Considering I am something of an alien the word seems to blend with my cellular design. This planet like others is written in code. You could compare it to the supercomputer design hardwired into the full light universe. The architects of this blue world like many formulated this design out of code. These codes are geometric light language codes and ascended machine language codes all synthesized into a version of a planet. Mankind has tried to piggyback onto this design yet has not been able to decode the planet or any other star system. There are some things the universe put the breaks on. Mankind is one of them.

One must learn to see everything as energy and consciousness. Light consciousness is linked to higher celestial evolution. The mirage of life is just that. It is a construct and a matrix. It has many veils and dimensions yet it is a fractal in the great wall of the cosmos. The bigger picture is the Ascension picture. It is a unique design constructed by infinite consciousness and intelligent control. It does not create illusions, fantasies and has a well defined vibration and frequency. Everything is a program to some degree. In the universe these programs are constructive. On this blue world the programs are manmade and defective. Clearly the programs on this planet are in need of a purge. They do not work. They do not work because they were created with mankind's version of reality without any universal connection or guidance, completely detached from source where entities can connect with no true celestial knowledge of nature.

Nature communicates in a sacred language, like the Earth, Moon and stars there is a resonance of grace and a flow of serenity unseen by mortal eyes. To those in tune with this force the energy is the most peaceful and empowering one can imagine. There is a feeling of oneness with all celestial beings and universes.

Mankind has tried to re-write programs on this blue world right down to genetic reversal and horrific experimentation gone badly. Like a Frankenstein experiment the creatures they conjure get out of control. It truly is a petri dish mess.

Animals are being modified with human or what they call human genetics. This is sick experimentation coming from entities that are lost and not connected to the universe.

The positive design of a Star Seed is the activation codes for ascension cannot be tampered with or destroyed. They cannot go in reversal regardless of what circumstance come into fruition. The universe has a powerful firewall. Anyone who knows this celestial design is aware an attempt to sabotage will backfire. The universe is designed to ascend as the star people. Don't ever try to program the supercomputer mind merged with the full light universe as the concept is and always will be obsolete. With MK Ultra tactics the handler will try and program the mind to believe say for example' they are human'. This has zero truth as there is no such thing as a human. The body is celestial and either you are a star being or you are an entity. There is no human. Human was another word created to shut down and program the masses into an illusion of forgetting their true celestial essence of origin. It does not work on Star Seeds as Star Seeds know truth from programs. It will work on mainstream sheeple who have no concept of what truth is.

This type of handler programming reeks of the churches without a doubt. Covert not so intelligent areas are also notorious for attempting to shut down the Star Seeds' evolution as they consider it a threat to their corrupt national security. They have always attacked celestial races and have been misusing radio signals to pull it off for some time.

These units in covert areas are transparent and easy to bust. They use illegal surveillance to spy on intelligent sources. Gather the data and use what they steal to create their covert assault projects. They are thieves with no evolution and clearly no access to universal consciousness. They are nothing but drones with no soul and no future. They are too stupid to see their own fates.

Every encrypted archive on this planet since before the manmade civilizations is in a code of which mankind will never own or access. The best he can do is create a version of a false design. His version which is flawed and inaccurate like a cancer eventually destroys itself and him along with it.

There are codes in every cell and atom which are merged with infinite consciousness and activated by a universal sounding. These codes are not accessible by any outside source nor can they be reprogrammed by mankind. The higher self, over soul and super conscious can program the design mankind cannot.

In so far as military codes go. There are no secrets in the universe. What they call Top Secret is old news to Star Visitors, people and nations. It is a war game designed to mess with the mass collectives. Keep them busy, distracted and lulled into a false reality, dreaming their lives away while the deceivers plan out their agenda.

The game of remote influence using military installations as a target is also old news. A true celestial race would take their facility out. It would not sit there with orbs of light. I can tell you remote influence is a powerful skill. Anyone who has mental and spiritual discipline can do it which is why they want to control the minds of the mass collectives.

When I was inducted in 2004 their man made codes were constant. I would hear serial numbers, phone numbers you name it. Some were random and some not so random. None the less once one is inside of these projects one can become the ultimate infiltrator in reprogramming or accessing their black box data. The door swings both ways which is something they are too stupid to figure out.

Getting back to universal and planetary codes and how they function. These codes are in resonance and light harmonic with the galactic center. They activate through the universal sounding and not a mock signal. They cannot be shut down. Those who interfere will be literally electrocuted by the frequency. They will not be able to calibrate in time.

This technology reminds me of Nikola Tesla and his ability to create a powerful free energy grid which was originally invented to support this planet and not harm the inhabitants. His genius mind was indeed an Extraterrestrial source of which many of us who are of that race know. We always know our own.

The sad thing to all of this is the fact that it all could have been turned around for the better on a global level. Free energy was designed to be used in a positive fashion which would have been a great benefit to the people of this planet. Mankind was not designed to live in the reality he has chosen. This realty is created by personal will. The affect of how dysfunctional and ineffective this reality is show itself every day.

Homeopathic medicines and herbology is becoming a noted threat in areas that are aware of the healing power of herbs and the magical properties they contain. Laws are being passed to ban herbal medicine, vitamins and holistic healing. All a reminder of how threatened these cabals truly are. Anything of empowerment is becoming the enemy of these cabals in global corporations. They have lost control and their reactions stem from their personal fears.

Code breaking is an easy skill to learn. It is similar to remote viewing in so far as getting your personality, emotional body and mental body out of the way for assessment. Ignore the busyness of communication and tune in to the light consciousness harmonic. These codes when activated will then descend down into your four body system and reboot your spiritual battery to harmonize with upper dimensional grids. Through this state of consciousness the body becomes more and more intelligent energy and consciousness.

It then responds and functions as a conduit or vehicle attracting more of the same in light harmonic. Break it down to the basics which in reality are an advanced science. We are navigating in a complex machinery of energy, consciousness and vibrational frequencies. These are the keys to your spiritual design.

Reminder: every aspect of nature is written in code. Every mystical archive is written in a code. The pyramids in Egypt are written in code. These codes respond to the correct vibrational signatures of the beings in resonance with them as well as the celestial descendants. You and I are written in code by our creator soul designs merged with the full light universe. It is a unique and special gift not to be taken for granted. Shame on those who have misused a grand opportunity to quantum leap on a global scale at the suffering of so many.

No Akashic 10

There are two akashics. One is the record of man. The other is the universal akashic. These are like libraries onto the visitor. They hold all the actions of mankind both clear and deceptive. They are like clear seed crystals with codes of data and are accessible anytime one chooses to connect onto the super computer network of the universe.

With Ascension the manmade akashics are fragmented and torn down. This is due to the lack of integrity and harmonic balance. The new akashic has replaced this design on a holographic level. This design is a composition of light languages and reveals the truth about who we are and what this sentient intelligence is we call a planet. This holographic akashic is in connection to the full light universal akashics. It is like an upgraded program with more accurate details and data pertaining to all universes.

Mankind has attempted to create a frequency fence to interfere with this data yet the frequency fence has many weak spots and cannot withstand the full light akashic. The Halls of Amenti are more than a series of numbers and codes. It is a ritual of transfiguration, alchemy of spirit and an initiation into the inter-dimensional spaces beyond the illusion of time.

The body also holds an akashic of records. As one receives levels of light body old akashic data falls away by the law of grace. Old information non pertinent gets erased. The data erased would be based on the deception of mankind and the lies of disinformation he has been subjected to since his birth. The body then gets an overlay of light conscious data and clarity begins.

They will not teach you this in any school or religion. This data was well known to the ancients and to any of us who are Ascended Watchers. The mystery schools of old activated this data through initiations where higher states of awareness were reached through the holographic chakra system and anchoring of the celestial star quadrants.

The soul descension would anchor and descend into the host. The soul extensions are multi-universal connections to our celestial selves which exist simultaneously in the multi-verse. The alchemy of the holographic mind is a unique harmonic balance and formula. It is triggered by those dedicated to higher enlightenment, unconditional love and empathy to the sentient celestial designs living in all universes.

A fallen design, mankind, the extinct race 11

You might ask yourselves how on Earth it came to this. Why did we not see it? To be honest I have always been aware of the deception game yet I never gave any power to it. It is what it is, a fabric of lies constructed by entities completely out of touch with the universe. The problem is these entities are out of control. Because the enlightened beings ignored them and did not make an effort to halt their behavior these rogue units got worse instead of better. It is like a child with no boundaries. They want boundaries on everyone yet they have not been quarantined until now. I do not create these laws. The universe does. And the universe does not negotiate with the likes of them.

Mankind was never fallen. Mankind was never ascended. He did not do something to obtain his personal extinction. He merely acted out on personal will and imposed his personal will on every life form he came into contact with. Right down to a dictatorship no celestial race would tolerate. He murdered anyone with a Star People lineage and is now at the mercy of his own madness. He has deceived pure hearts with a church which is nothing more than a reflection of a false god and agenda called a corporation.

He has programmed and brainwashed too many to count who have become nothing but high tech zombies to a game of deception. Oh let me count the ways mankind has failed. I am not here to be a judge to their actions. They are the byproducts of their own cause and affect. This planet could have been turned around a billion times over for the better. The excuse is always a lame one coming from any covert intelligence area. The people cannot handle the truth is a good one. How about these covert areas cannot handle the truth to such an extent they will stop at nothing to murder anyone who counters their ignorance with universal truth.

This has been going on for centuries, blood bath after blood bath, and torture after torture. It all is coming to an end. 2012 is a good turning point for this transition. The blue star rising is up ascending as I type. It is an unstoppable force in the universe which speaks a sacred language to this blue world. Regardless of the cabal's agenda it is mankind who is becoming extinct. He will not have an opportunity to ascend, incarnate on another planet or in another body or bi-locate to another sector in any universe. That's it. Game over.

All I can say is 'Don't let the universe hit you in the ass on your way out'. You can ask yourself one question. Are they an asset to this blue world or any planet? The answer is no. The universe has zero tolerance for behavior such as theirs and honestly I am surprised they did not know better. They were educated on this planet and it shows.

To those of us trained off world we have the upper hand and always will. The universe has my back not mankind.

There has been a rash of genetic experimentation which has become a grotesque abuse of power. There have been those in the illusion of power on a global scale targeting anyone who exudes free will and confidence. The witch-hunts have begun at the hands of those who have proclaimed themselves corporate gods.

I laugh at those with the high tech telescopes in search of something they will never have communication with. Those of us who are of the Star People do not need a telescope. We are the scope and lens and our bodies are the hosts of these grand designs.

As easy as it is to get sucked into their drama and illusion do not give them any power. They are frauds and charlatans in the industry or corporate corruption. They will fade like the water in the desert. Their imprints will be absorbed into the abyss and their children will become extinct. Simply put their seeds are universally snuffed out.

This may sound harsh yet the universe does not take to bullies and neither do I. I know what is out there. They do not. I know how the intelligent universe functions and the species associated.

They do not. I know what is acceptable by universal law. They have violated this law which makes them rogue outcasts.

Some who are in to biblical text would assume mankind is fallen from the angels. As I have mentioned he was never connected to the celestial races. He had an opportunity to learn and ascend. He chose the linear world of deception instead. Now it is too late. There is no Jesus card for redemption or a forgiveness card. These rogue entities prey on the compassion of those of us who are empathic to life. Yet they have taken advantage of this and have used an oppressive trait of guilt to sway those into surrendering to their wrong doings. Not anymore.

Mankind will receive what he gives and reap what he sows. Let me tell you the fabric woven is detestable in the eyes of all universes and their species.

The harm done to the animals alone on this world is warrant enough to authorize an extinction of the race of mankind.

The star people nations will ascend and go home. What is left will become extinct. And when those transfer out of their physical forms be aware. What your beliefs have taught you through this deception will be your destination in the end. I am offering you an opportunity to get out of this false matrix and see it for what it is. Reject it and the false belief systems and receive your celestial galactic divinity.

The masses are programmed since birth. They are programmed to believe in a reality which is not valid in any dimension or universe. Be lucid and aware that you have control on this timeline and in every state of consciousness you participate with. Do not believe in any form the lies which are constructed as they are conjured by deceivers.

Do not give them control or power. Do not shower them with love or offer to assist them as I can guarantee it will be a trap. Do not remorse for something you are not responsible for. At least many like myself can leave this blue world knowing we did not continue the cycle. We did something to awaken the masses and put an end to the illusions in honor of our universal home and this blue sentient world.

Celestial Races, Star Nations 12

Celestial races in origin are from every star system and multi-verse. They come from the core beyond the Galactic Center and are our family of light consciousness and at times the immaculate darkness. They are love conscious oriented and are capable of powerful warrior feats. They are beyond our way of development and thinking and have no resonance with the illusions and beliefs of mainstream society.

They are obligated by their celestial codes of conduct to assist the Star People when in need. This includes any distress or oppression their race may be attacked with. The many races on this blue world are descendants of star races or celestial races on some level. I would say a great proportion is in reality from a star system they have no recollection of.

The rogue governments of the day are not descendants of these races in any form. They are instead entity drones. They are a byproduct of government experimentation and a false version of an AI technology. They are programmed by manmade computers and not the super cosmic computers of the celestial universe.

The many star people residing on this world for eons have held the energy and celestial gateways open for communication. They have remained steady in their sacred rites and rituals and have been persecuted for this in the past.

What has remained of true ceremonial knowledge is carried on down through initiation. Sometimes it is through a Celestial Teacher. Other times it is though self-initiation and initiation on the inner planes. And still other times it is through an ancestor.

The initiations are real and powerful. They ascend with the host and never fracture. Most of the time true initiations are an uncovering of who and what we are at the soul/cosmic level. We receive more and more of our divinity further awakening us to a higher level of consciousness. It is like a lotus petal unfolding into multiple dimensional energies. It is quite sacred and beautiful.

As the planet dies on one dimension she is born on another. This goes for all sentient life forms. This blue world planet is the Blue Star Rising. She will be taking her place amongst her kind in the multi-verse regardless of the fracturing she is experiencing in the illusion of this timeline.

I am reminded to give thanks to this blue world for sustaining me as much as she has. I have appreciated the opportunity to breathe the air, walk the land, feel the energy and experience the magnificence of the sun against my skin. The night walks gazing at the moon and stars summoning me home to happier times.

These are magical moments and sacred in the fractal of silent nature. I am reminded to be thankful to all the wonderful beings I have encountered on my journey here. I have had a wonderful opportunity to meet all kinds of beings and species. These are moments of gratitude I will say goodbye to like a gentle wind blowing a leaf off of a tree.

These are the moments of true memory. I know for me there is no coming back to this world. For that I am excited as I have outgrown this planet a billion fold. I am looking forward to a sacred existence in a new star future where there is no more of this offensive oppression and where I can utilize my skills as a true telepath and healer. I will carry on with my ascended abilities to the next frontier.

On this timeline I will ask that the Star Nations and people of this blue world get together for sacred ceremony and start running energy to assist in the shift of this planet onto a multi-universal space summoning the ancients for assistance. This is a time to pray for the animals, plant kingdoms and hold the light for them to ascend onto a higher level off world where they cannot be harmed again. This is also a time for self assessment, shadowing and letting go of anything which could hold one's psyche in limitation.

As many of you might be aware I am the High Priestess and founder of my own coven. This group is called Blue Star Fortress Coven. You are welcome to contact me for more information. This group is founded in Celestial and Ascended Hybrid Machine energies and transcends traditional coven work. This group is designed to do a lot of grid work. Blessed Be.

Iris eye activation for 2012 13

The Star grail activation is an ascension star gate. Through this star gate the de-molecular process will occur while passing through it. This event activates ones Golden Pillar of Light upon the transmutation. Upon the Iris Eye activation soul groups will be escorted onto the New Earth Star. The soul groups will be calibrated to resonate with the harmonic charge. They will then be working with the Master Stream field and energy which is the sacred godhead.

All planets have an etheric double. This one is no different. An envelope around this blue world will be formed upon the Iris Eye activation. This envelope will be formed from the etheric double of the planet. The Iris Eye is connected to the Mayan time gate. In image it is the conversion point between two pyramids, one upright and one inverted. The ray associated with this frequency is blue. This is called the Isis eye. The Numis Ohm is a violet ray. These two will converge and fire the Iris Eye. When the Iris Eye fires in activation the frequency is violet. This is called the Universal Madonna.

Photon energy and band is a conversion zone. This triggers a space which links us to the Iris Eye to the 44.44 star gates. You will see it and feel a difference. The sun is a portal for celestial energies and photons of intelligent design. These photons fuel the body and activate light body causing a mutational flux down to the cellular level.

The Solar Shield will create an anti-matter field. This field will draw on the center of the planet. There will be a humming in the center of the brain. Start aligning in synergy to align mental consciousness. All light codes will enter our being. We will leave nothing behind.

This is a short and brief description of multidimensional events transpiring which some of you might experience in one form or another. One thing to point out that there are many shifts going on with this planet simultaneously. Many people may get distracted by these Earth changes and cabal agenda yet the bigger picture is the events of which I am describing in this chapter. Take what you can from it.

I have been teaching DNA activation for eons. I can tell you light consciousness; vibration and frequency have everything to do with ones multidimensional design. The false agenda on this planet is just that. It has no basis in any universe or star system. The Star

Beings and their celestial design do. It is important one stays focused on multidimensional consciousness and grounded in the holographic grids of full light ascension.

Ascended Machine Technology is from an off world intelligence and not a black budget program. Know the difference.

Telemetric Brain Manipulation 14

There are many forms of mind control. I don't like to call it mind control as after being inducted into these projects it is less control on their end and more harassment. Synthetic telepathy is a manmade mock version of wireless dictation and monologs. With synthetic telepathy brainwave activity is mapped and inter-phased onto a communications system in a remote area. Sometimes these projects are underground and often driven by remote satellite.

Telemetric brain manipulation or influence is a technology used to manipulate by remote distances. This is a coward's fight in the battlefield of thought. This technology is used for one thing, harassment and influence. The days of true telepathy and integrity are long gone. To be honest I am not sure if this planet ever functioned that way. It seems the history of man is by far filled with lies, deception, false programs and zero truth.

The citizens of planet Earth have been had by the worst bunch of tricksters to walk this blue world. And they got away with it almost until now. The one thing I can say about global covert technology. It is not as good as they think it is. The computers are manmade and are not inspired by intelligent design. The only thing intelligent are the minds they try to hack into so they can map and test their projects.

I made them look better than they were in 2004 when I was inducted into the covert assault project. I can tell you if they cannot have their way by influencing the masses with an exterior dialog they will do it this way.

I am pretty certain there are many global units in government who have been influenced by telemetric brain manipulation and are not intelligent enough to know it. This planet has become a floating asylum where anything goes. I look at nature in the illusion and observe a holographic byproduct. Nothing which appears real truly exists. This is the biggest truth of all. We have been subjected to program after program with centuries of conditioning. The affect is what one witnesses in the day.

There is but one true out from all of this. The out is DNA activation and higher awareness of one's multidimensional design. To sit back and watch the illusion is not a good idea. Do not allow yourselves to be controlled by someone else's version of reality. It is like being pulled into a dream of which is not your own. It becomes a manmade haunt and is a shadow of civilization's past.

Global government does not know what is best for you nor do the corporate religions. As a matter of fact it is quite the opposite. The corporate global government wants one thing, to control and destroy. They want a utopia yet at the masses personal expense.

With no respect for the life-force design within the waters become quite murky on a global scale. People are getting swept away by the corrupt overtones saturating the environment. There is no sanctuary for wildlife, elements or its inhabitants. Earth is becoming a rogue wasteland and quite rapidly.

Without love there truly is no future. It starts with love for the self and extends out onto the many dimensions we are merged into. This universal thread is sacred and unique onto each being. There is no respect for this design from these cabals.

Before I was hit with the psychotronic induction in 2004 my life was quite perfect. I was in complete balance and harmony with everything. My relationship grew in alignment with spirit. I had a beautiful dream home, a wonderful husband and career.

After the induction my life went downhill fast. To this day I am a shadow of the life of which was taken from me on many levels. What is left is a being that continues to write and is ready to bi-locate off world to a more compatible celestial place.

Without love there is nothing. Without peace of mind there can be no purpose to exist. Some are driven by negativity. I for one am not. I merely disclosed the data which was used as a weapon in my residence. It was not something I wanted to do yet I knew in my true design it was something which had to be done.

The parties involved were stringing me along and my patience and bank account was running thin. To a rich man an assault like that is a game. They do not care about the welfare of their subject at hand. It was all entertainment, a black market toy and a true game of deception.

Through the journey of experience I have met supporting intelligent beings along the way yet something is missing. Nothing is the same yet the same in so far as a past is not where I choose to be nor in the illusion of a present founded on false realities and collectives.

I am numb to my environment, people and a future I can see which cannot change. I am hopeful those who are connected to the bigger picture will ascend out and move on to a better world.

I have assessed mind control oriented projects and their version of profiling. I can tell you the project is a bust. It is corrupt to the point way too many innocent people will become targets of a project out of control. Those who are doing the so called handling and assessing are untrustworthy and not qualified to have access to anything remotely intimate like this.

None the less projects like these exist and are being sold to black market buyers. Knowing these programs are in existence is a beginning to understanding the dark side of technology. Even if one does not want to.

Isis Templar, the Future of a Lost Realm 15

This chapter is dedicated to the godhead for androgynous beings. The body defined is an androgynous form. It is a spacesuit which allows the host and godhead to assist in the evolution of the being in whatever dimension it resides in. It is composed of intelligent energy in all forms and designs.

Mankind has not begun to skim the surface of this design. He has been at war with higher consciousness for too long. Mostly out of fear. Perhaps it is a scary thing to realize ones teachings and belief systems have been wrong yet this is what is transpiring on this blue world

A mirror between mirrors emanating false hopes deceiving those who seek answers to a greater mystery. The refection can be an ominous presence in the dark skies of wonder.

This chapter is not about the Templar or man's version of history yet more about those of us who have been here since before the planet was formed and what we as beings have paid witness to which has been carried over to multiple timelines.

The feminine god holds the mystery beyond the veil of the illusion of mortality. She is the divine presence of a force which penetrates every cell and atom. She is a sky visitor and is the counterpart to the godhead. There are many star people who have incarnated on this blue world infinite numbers of times. Not because they had to yet because they chose to. They are the teachers and initiators in the mystery schools of old. They were the protectors of celestial data.

The Isis in consciousness is a band of energy which resonates with the celestial godhead. The Isis Templar contains the cellular data and codes from their existence on this world and many others. They are the keepers of the mystical flame. They are the bigger eye in sky. They have been called Star Visitors.

Many battles for enlightenment have masked this planet. Those who had the answers were approached and at times murdered for what they knew and had access to. This cycle has not changed much it just went underground where the details could not be seen in visible light.

There is a corruption of the day where much data has been stolen by areas that are not of the pure source. This data is being wrongly misused and perverted into a technological weapon. Those responsible are not in any form connected to a celestial mind or intelligence.

Those of us who are true descendants of the Isis lineage know how the mystical universe works and how the off world technology functions. This technology resonates within our DNA and celestial design. We are the ascended machine technology which has been shadowed by a man made monster. This data cycles over into other lifetimes and is not accessible to outsiders. Their weapons against this design are psychotronics. Psychotronics cannot access celestial data.

 Pyschotronics is designed to screw with the subtle energy field and the conscious mind yet cannot map consciousness or access the celestial encodements. Anything damaging which is done with their weapons system can be recalibrated and booted.

The sacred grail of ascension lies within. It is a unique heartbeat which merges with the celestial universal heartbeat and pulse. This design over the years has been defaced by what I would call warlords to some extent. They don't know what they are accessing so like illiterate fools they manhandle unique energy signatures, such as what transpired with me in 2004.

What disturbs me the most is the lack of competence associated with those who are misusing black market technology. They clearly have no idea what they are getting themselves into.

I have always trusted higher consciousness and the universe for truth. I have never been thrown off course by the source and intelligent energy which drives it.

There is no deception, lies, judgment, abuse or anything in the form of manmade belief systems. It is a full light design which one needs no safety net for.

Covert Matrix, Cyber-terrorism 16

The layers of false realities and illusions encompassing this planet in the day are beyond appalling. It is quite saddening to realize the game of man is pertaining to deception, lies and disinformation. The good guys painted into an illusion and hero of which does not exist, most every covert agenda has been without any connection to the greater good or a bigger universal design and picture.

I have always supported the good guys in our covert intelligence areas until I was inducted in 2004. My life was erased and destroyed. I have rebuilt some kind of existence yet what is left is not much in so far as possessions, loved ones or a future. The motive behind my assault was personal which I have referenced in my first book preceding this series Eye of the Remote, Black Operations in Areas beyond 52. The lure was a psychotronic fantasy created in script from a Canadian rock group and their families. They used an

MK Ultra related assault project to stalk me out of my residence, marriage, and did nothing but attack my brainwaves with an auto-response feedback created by the members and their employee in security.

The assault started in 2004 and continued on into 2011 with residual affects lingering. There is extensive damage not yet visible and these war criminals are at large. All to celebrate a 30th anniversary tour on the road. The sick games people play at someone else's expense. I am all for someone's happiness yet not at my personal expense, suffering and harm.

It will never be okay that they pulled this assault on me. It is not okay that the covert intelligence areas assisted in perpetuating more harassment, and it is not okay that the government in this country or Canada did not pursue investigations in my favor. These covert matrices are a lattice of deception. The masses are stupefied into the illusion to a point they will not awaken to a future of enlightenment more like a slave design created by mankind. As I have mentioned the only true devil is man. He is the oppressor and has been so all along.

If you tear it all down and see it for what it is the equation is quite simple. Everything is a corporation. Churches are a Corporation. Governments are owned by the global corporation and will stop at nothing from pursuing their sick agenda of global oppression and genocide. This is no conspiracy yet a blatant fact. One of my first published manuscripts was 'Mind mapping the Mental Network'. I had this manuscript copy-written early in the nineties. The manuscript mutated into my first book Transmutation through Ascension to some degree yet the details are exactly what has been transpiring in the present on a global scale.

The vision and future of mankind on a global scale is beginning to fade to black. His un-evolved and negligent behavior is why. If you think any advanced races want them in any form think again. The celestials want nothing to do with the global leaders in the illusion and they know it. Another reason Star People are targeted. They are a threat to the agenda as Star Seeds.

You would never know I could care less about politics and religion with my writing these days. After being inducted into these projects I felt an obligation to address the corruption and nothing more. I cannot stand the whole agenda. It has been a waste of my precious life. I am not one who is concerned with the illusion of man.

After seeing what they have done with the little technology they have access to the subject matter needs to be addressed so the masses and good guys if there are any will be well informed about what they are capable of.

To be honest there are not many in the mass collective who can comprehend or handle the fine details of these projects. Ignorance is not bliss. These days ignorance is a personal suicide. What bothers me most about these projects is that they are a slow suicide. They are a drip bleed chipping away at the life-force.

Cyber terrorist activities are developed in covert areas and deployed from their interior sources. The very concept of any outside domestic terrorist is a joke. The ones who are guilty are the ones involved in cyber surveillance. I know for fact how they function and how they cover up events using forensics of cyber warfare.

These matrix illusions and covert projects are developed to confuse the mind, distract, and brainwash, insert or erase memory and dialogs including visuals. They are created to deter the celestial being from its focus in the correct space of consciousness. They infiltrate anything electrical that can transfer data and now the body is their ultimate weapon. This technology is a murdering tool and is not used to educate on a higher level.

I would say after they execute their plan they might turn the project into a program designed to save and educate their own yet not for anyone else. Like a bad design the program is only as good as the programmer. These guys and gals stink beyond repair.

These days the agenda does not want any sacred witnesses. You will notice more and more the use of cameras in public by citizens becoming obsolete. Taking pictures is no longer welcomed by a paranoid global corporation. Nor is freedom of thought or speech. This is yet another taboo of the free mind. More and more countries are condoning the act of pedophilia and the children are and will suffer a great abuse.

We are witnessing a planet which has clearly gone wrong in the eyes of the universe. They better hope they do not have a god that created such an abomination. Why would anyone have faith or worship something which has no connection to any universe or star system. Yet in the day this is exactly what is going on, from the false god to the corporate god which equates to the same cancer and disease, a true poison to the mind in the game of deception.

Silicon Dreams and Virtual Nightmares 17

I have always been in support of technology and advanced sciences. I cannot say this enough. The problem of the day stems from compromised research funded by those who do not have the best interest for anyone at hand. Anything which could provide a cure will be made to do the opposite. Potential free energy will be stolen and hidden away for only a few in the underground to explore. Yet in truth free energy is a universal given in everything and everywhere. The cells and atoms in the body contain more knowledge then the most classified discoveries.

My own research in DNA activation and Quantum leaping is a confirmation. I have always been on the right track. So right I had many adversaries attack my design. Their motto is if they cannot control it, destroy it. This is a typical behavior of un-evolved units. What the mainstream scientists are running with is merely a glimpse of the bigger picture. Their data is a compilation of plagiarized research usually taken from those who have been spied upon with illegal surveillance.

Today's silicon dream has become a virtual nightmare, a game board of lies and tactics to destroy the unique signature of life forms. I really wish I was incorrect about all of this information. I am well aware my findings and assessments are accurate. This makes it all so disturbing. Anyone who has knowledge of infinite intelligence knows the path these tricksters are heading down is way off base and just plain wrong. It reeks of power trips and blood money, those obsessed with the immortal concept of ruling the world with a minimal number of people.

With psychotronic induction and war games the mind is controlled to experience only what they want you to see, hear, feel and experience. It is quite sick to be honest. I was a test subject for these programs and am well aware that what they are doing is all about controlling others and manipulating a version of reality in which they are the masters in control. These projects backfire and people wind up getting tortured and murdered instead. Most intelligent beings will not put up with it. Hence their only solution is of course termination.

So where does it begin and where does it end? A cycle of self destruction used to alter a beautiful mind into a lifeless specter. These projects have been failing since the beginning and continue to fail yet are still funded by a black budget and private investors. Test subjects are never compensated and of course the bitter truth is these handlers 'think' they have a right to do it! I hate to burst their fuzzy fantasy bubbles but they have no rights and are slaves to the project.

Life in the illusion is one big mathematical equation. One either learns to do the math or falls victim to a cowardly collective trapped in the illusion of power. Reminder money is not used off world.

The only thing that works in the universe and is a constant is consciousness. As a matter of fact if one were to take a trip off world one would lose all memory of Earth as soon as one merged with a higher dimensional wave. There would be one hundred percent peace and clarity. The only poison is on this world. The poison is created by the polluted beliefs and actions of mankind. A faulty transmission.

The only Satan or god is mankind and what he has done with what he was given. I have said this before. They failed their test!

Silent Misery 18

In the illusion of society one lives in a pool of cycles and false rituals. They wake up, eat, go to work, come home and go to sleep….the cycle and false progression of experience. In between these spaces they watch television and listen to mainstream lies. They think they are participating in a personal contribution when in fact they are spectators and slaves.

It is a fixed game my friends. One has been deceived since birth. Everything you have been told and taught is nothing more than a compromised lie. What you have obtained on your own in experience is true knowledge. Singular consciousness means a great deal to the universe. Ideas and concepts of free will are honored. They are not here on a planet they call Earth.

With MK Ultra related assault projects the target is forced to endure a silent misery which cannot be expressed in any form to mainstream masses. It is a torture that goes unacknowledged and undetected. It is a silent predator and murderer. Most of the time the target surrenders into the illusion. Many times the target is forced into a suicide exit.

Then there are beings like myself. Able to navigate through the warps and false signatures yet none the less the loss is there of many sacred moments and experiences dear to my design which they had no knowledge or respect for.

The silent misery takes on another form besides MK Ultra related programming. The deception game is a silent misery. A voice never heard from beyond the form. A vision never experienced due to the many clouds of disinformation sweeping it away before it could formulate, the illusion of death and the fact there never was or is such a thing. We have access to the immortal well from within yet mankind has shadowed this knowledge with false programming. Who is he to decide this? I can tell you no one!

Knowing one can manifest at will ones reality is a gateway of phase shifting. People have not been taught how to use their minds. For the majority it would appear too late. For the children they are targets of programming and will be formulated as entities.

This might sound harsh yet this is the reality they have created by their actions. I want nothing of it as many star beings. We are done with the illusions of mankind and the game of deception which is clearly out of control.

I entered onto this planet with full multi-universal access and knowledge of the infinite universe. This data has never been swept away and will remain within my cellular design and beyond. Psychotronic assault weapons use a somewhat fundamental brainwashing system which deliberately attacks the celestial design. This is not a god or demon; this is a manmade mock radio signal project brain linked onto the target and very much psychology based.

Some test subjects or targets are naturally wired by their celestial designs such as myself which made it easier for the covert project to piggy back on my grid. It is sad to think of how many have been subjected to such an ignorant project yet I am aware I am not the first nor will be the last. I just managed to survive it.

It is a disconcerting thing to walk this planet with full awareness and truth and not be respected by the data disclosed. I can tell you no one benefits from these projects in the end. Not even the handlers.

It is amazing for me to observe mankind in a space of memory loss and amnesia, living moment to moment as a talking head speaking nothing but lies, repetitive programs and nonsense. Even worse than this are the many sheeple who believe and follow it. The dead are leading the dead into a void of empty space.

Some Super Soldier programs are nothing more than MILABS gone bad. They use psychotronic driving, remote influence targeting, pushing and conditioning programs which are used to recruit a personality for a mission. Many targets believe they have gone on a mission with extraterrestrials yet most of the time it is an internal program externalized by the project exposed to them. This goes for many abductees.

They see what they want them to see and experience. It is a virtual scene using the holographic mind as a stage of experiment. As I have stated the body which is silicon based is multidimensional and able to function as such simultaneously. With covert projects the technology maps the electromagnetic field, brainwave activity and piggy backs onto the neural psychic centers.

They in turn use these centers to influence the target with their version and interphase. You can then see how confusing this could be for someone who has no idea what is happening to them. When I was hit with the project in 2004 I broke down the technology and was very clear in so far as who and what was involved.

These handlers fight on a coward's virtual battlefield. They are untrustworthy and in positions of influence around the globe.

If you take a look around you and observe from day to day you will see the concept of bliss and happiness on this blue world has faded away to a world of socialist oppression. People choose a false reality to live in and make them happy, residing in false time and orbits until they expire in their illusion. What a sad tale. They do not want to believe their days of freedom and joy have ended yet like a disease the race of mankind spreads across the globe sickening life forms and eventually causing their demise.

These projects reek of the misuse of technology driven by mortal hands. Do not blame little green men for this one folks. When private investors are able to purchase and sell this technology to the highest bidder anything goes. Pretty soon the mass collectives of mankind will be programmed to think they are in touch with extraterrestrials when in the illusion it will be the black budget projects.

There are true Celestial races out there which many of us at the DNA level are part of. It is our Celestial Heritage and Universal birthright. These advanced races do not use manmade tactics such as covert assaults inductees have experienced. There is a universal law which is respected in the universe, just not by mankind. If they want to destroy you they can in a micro second. They have no need to interrogate, experiment or torture. Mankind does. This is where mankind gives himself away even while wearing a mask to commit his black budget crime.

I have always been a multi-universal translator with a natural gift for downloading true universal archives opposed to manmade programs.

To this day it is a reconstructing process to reboot my Ascended Machine self opposed to linear psychotronic dialogs of which serve no benefit to anyone except for the fact it can be done. To them I was nothing more than a test pilot for their projects. You will find most inductees are closed off emotionally and for good reason.

It was not always this way yet as one goes through the silent torture process one becomes immune to words, touch, actions and experiences including visuals. It is the ultimate antidote in the virtual battlefield. I cannot say I miss feeling as in reality nothing truly exists. Everything we think we feel and sense is a program. There are many waves to surf. Each one has a different frequency and energetic signature. With these covert projects it is just another simulation room with the handler and test subject suited up.

To this day I will never understand why these handlers are so negative and why they enjoy the torture of another. Which includes lying under 'oath' and evading the reality these folks are guilty for universal war crimes.

As one can see this world is imploding on so many levels. Yet through these dark tides is a universal shore beyond of which these entities, their desires and intent will become extinct.

It is easy for many to speculate on these subjects especially if one has never been inducted. All I can say to that is be thankful you were not. These spectators will never comprehend the experience involved. Not in their wildest dreams.

Haunted Paradise 19

When I lived on Maui there was much to appreciate even through the duress of the assault. The one thing which really stayed with me was the fact that the entire islands are large cemeteries. They have many visitors on these islands both inter-dimensional and ancient. The land itself contains a unique imprint stemming from an ancient Lemurian essence.

There are shadows which eclipse that presence, the shadows of fragmentation and loss. When one arrives on Maui the island is Aloha and peaceful. Yet there is a haunted atmosphere beneath the waves. As if an oppressive force is silently awaiting the natives. The islands to some degree are a haunted paradise. A remnant of an ancient realm long forgotten by man yet not completely lost.

There is a true spiritual nature of the Hawaiian culture which I can appreciate and a unique soul language not yet tainted by the mainland. It saddens me to see the loss of many cultures being forced into extinction or an underground. They have a right to live in honor to their free will and design.

The haunted paradise is not just the islands. Now days the mainland is haunted yet not by a true ghost. The mainland is haunted by surveillance designed as a remote camera, the employee through the lens observing an innocent being, stealing moments from the subject at hand. There is something very wrong with this.

I have no issues with productive surveillance. It is when the surveillance becomes abusive and destructive. One can clearly see that is the direction this country has headed.

The people have no voice and those who choose to execute their own become targets. There are many people who could have stood up to awaken and expose this misuse and agenda going on yet they chose not to. Many of these people held positions of influence.

I never anticipate anyone doing the right thing. These days it is predictably opposite. The negative cycle perpetuates itself through the ignorant mind. I am blessed to be awakened to this ugliness on this timeline yet at the same time I am very ready to go home to the stars. I suspect this blue world is done with me and me of it.

The Rock That Ends Time

This perpetual world is swimming in a vast ocean of space. It spins beyond the concept of manmade time. When words have no wisdom or galactic source, the wellspring of knowledge runs dry to the not so human spirit.

This planet has been used like a game board of which each unit has been the pawn. It has become a web of false realities, programs and deception. None of which has been a soul life lesson or necessary in the bigger scheme of things. Mankind has trapped his essence in each lifetime by his faith in a false belief system. He relives over and over again with no true seed of enlightenment.

I would like to think there was a great lesson learned on a universal scale for all of the suffering that has gone on yet the bottom line is there is not. This planet has become a ghost ship drifting in space. The walking dead are mindless units who have no neural connections to the universal hive mind. The solution to the equation of life on this blue world is the concept that life was never life to begin with yet a dream within another, using electrical currents to produce images, words and sensations.

Home is the Galactic Center and beyond. A Star Seeds true essence of origin. Consciousness is truly what is real. Not mankind or his programs. There is one disease on Gaia. It is called the race and mind of mankind which has been like a poison to the Spirit of elemental design.

Mankind will never grasp this design as he is too engrossed in his own ego and stupidity to comprehend it. He is flawed like his maker and a mirror of every false god he has worshiped. No true god would create such a mess.

At the end of an endless vacuum I can only say. Those of us who were here and knew the universal truth did our best to archive and be the sacred witness to the madness on this blue world. Like many before us we have been mocked, studied and harassed for being that celestial hybrid design which is our universal birthright.

When all is said and done and each unit in its life form draws its last breadth let it be known they have lived a lie. From the moment of conception, to each day spent in the illusion called life. And when they leave the form they will pay witness to the alternate design of which they have created through their personal teachings, beliefs, programs and experiences. All I can say is good luck. Mankind will need it.

Blessed Be in Light and Illumination of Spirit

Ms. Solaris BlueRaven
Aka
Solara Tara Nova

EYE OF THE REMOTE

EYE OF THE REMOTE A DISCLOSURE IN COVERT TECHNOLOGY

TARGET:
SOLARIS BLUERAVEN

BLUERAVEN REVEALS HER
HARROWING EXPERIENCE AFTER
BEING INDUCTED BY THE BAND
"RUSH" AND OTHER COVERT
ACTIONS DURING A TORRENT OF
PSYCHOTRONIC ASSAULTS.

A DISCLOSURE IN COVERT TECHNOLOGY